PRECIOUS

PRECIOUS

A Collection of Poems
(Second Edition)

Onyinye Oyedele

iUniverse, Inc.
Bloomington

PRECIOUS
A COLLECTION OF POEMS (SECOND EDITION)

iUniverse books may be ordered through booksellers or by contacting:

iUniverse
1663 Liberty Drive
Bloomington, IN 47403
www.iuniverse.com
1-800-Authors (1-800-288-4677)

ISBN: 978-1-4620-2797-2 (pbk)
ISBN: 978-1-4620-2796-5 (ebk)

Printed in the United States of America

iUniverse rev. date: 06/17/2011

DEDICATION

To the Almighty God,
The giver of life and the one
Who makes all things beautiful in *His time.*

CONTENTS

CHRISTMAS

LIFE

FAMILY

SYNOPSIS

Precious is a collection of poems from everyday life. It is written in a style that captures cherished moments: *Faith, People, Roots, Love, Places & Sights, Motherhood, Christmas, Life, and Family.*

Precious is a collage of images and scenes from Europe, Africa, and North America. It will make you laugh, cry, pause, and ask, "What are the "***Precious***" things in my life?"

FAITH

MY RESORT

Lord please teach me how to be still-
My day runs off and I play catch up.
My mind races across the piles of dishes
My mind races across the loads of laundry
My mind races across the meals to prepare
My mind races to the grocery store,
Lord please let my mind race to you.
Let me find solitude amidst the day's chaos
Lead me to a hiding place;
Where my heart can cry out in desperation for you
Lord you are my hiding place
You are my resort!

BEAUTIFUL FEET

Lord, I thank you for shoes to wear
For the warmth, comfort, and good deals!
Oh yes, those numerous "feet enticers" I must learn to say
no to!
But Lord, I thank you for sandals and slippers in the
summer . . . wow!
Thank you for the sun rays kissing my feet,
Thank you for the sand and gravel rubbing my soles.
Above all, Lord, please let my feet be "beautiful feet"
May I bring good news, peace, and joy wherever I go
Please guide my feet and lead me on the right path
Lord please order my steps, you know I am prone to haste!
As the sunshine gives light to my toes, please light my path
now and always.
Please protect and deliver me from slips and falls
Thank you for willing and able feet to do your biddings!
Lord, I thank you once again for my "faithful" shoes
And I ask for joy to freely give away some when you beckon . . .
hmm yes lord.

PUT ON

Lord, I thank you for the beautiful seasons of life
I thank you for the brightness of summer
I thank you for the colours of autumn
I thank you for the blossoming flowers in spring
And lord I thank you for the wonder of snow in winter!
Hmmm
I thank you for the privilege to see the wonder of your hands.
I thank you for the clothes you have provided to cover me every season
I thank you for the men and women gifted in dress making.
Today as I choose an outfit to put on
May I also remember to put on your virtues . . .
Oh, please may I put on truth, love, joy, kindness, and patience
Please help me to put on honesty, long suffering, meekness, and forgiveness
May I "dress" to fit the "weather" of my day and its challenges
May I "dress" to enjoy the gift of today and all that it will deliver;
Oh, please give me the garment of praise!
Lord, I thank you once again for the clothes in my closet
But above all, please let me look more into your closet
And put on your choices for my life.

WHEN SAINTS ARE GONE

We cry and we hurt when loved ones go
We are tempted to ask "why God why?"
We hurt so deeply, we lose our strength
When saints are gone it is all right to cry.

We remember their sweetness
Their voices echo in our head and heart
We still see them on our screen and albums,
But we know that they believed in the Almighty.

We know that they did what they were called to do here
We must pause in our sorrows to celebrate them,
Because they dared to launch into the deep
And spread their belief.
When saints are gone
They believed in someone high above
And so we must believe so one day we can unite . . .

WORSHIP

I get on my knees,
I lay flat on my face
I am lost in your presence,
Sometimes my heart and mind wander
I struggle with keeping my focus on you
But I know I will be blessed
Just because I came.

I wish I could be more regular
Coming to you before dawn
Just before the hustle and bustle of the day begins
Help me Lord, because that is my desire
I am tired of giving you the crumbs of my day
You deserve the whole loaf.
Let my heart long to worship you each moment
Teach me how to hide from the cares of this world,
In your presence Lord, I find strength for each day.

HEALING

Not just for the blind, deaf, and dumb
But also for the broken hearted,
The rejected and despised.
Not only for the sick, lame, and crippled
But also for the bruised, abused, and betrayed.
Healing is for everyone.
Healing, healing, healing.

For everyone that is hurting
For everyone that has experienced pain
For everyone who has been left alone
In the cold by family or friends
Moments when they turned their back on you
And made your heart sink . . .
Healing and mercy, your daily vitamins for moving on.

Healing of the heart,
Healing of the mind
Healing of the body
Healing of the soul.
Knitted and intertwined with forgiveness,
Inseparable partners
In a world, filled with so much pain
Healing is a need in our world today.

ONE DAY

In all the hustling and bustling
In all the chaos and troubles
One day, my Saviour will come
One day, He will appear.

In all the disasters and tragedies
In all the pains and wounds
He will come with healing in His wings
He will come with peace in His wings
One day might be my Lord's day.

We don't know the day or time
We don't know the moment or season
It could be in the morning, noon or evening
One day could be any day.

SISTERS

When we pray together
Our hearts become one
When we share our burdens
Our hearts become one,
We are sisters talking to our Father!

On the phone, we will pray
In our homes, we will pray
In our car we will pray.
In fellowship, we will join hands and pray
You are my sisters and I am not ashamed to say
I need you to pray for me;
We are sisters talking to our Father.

We are connected by divine love
We are united by divine peace
You are my sisters by His unique blood
We belong to the family of God . . .

Dedicated to **_Ladies Share and Care,_**
City Center Baptist Church, Mississauga, Ontario, Canada.

PEOPLE

WHEN YOU DARE TO CARE

When you open your arms and love a stranger
When you give food and shelter to one in need
When you dare to care
You change the world,
One life at a time.

When you help to shape a life
When you help to give hope and courage
When you help to set boundaries and influence change
When you dare to care for another life
You are making a difference,
You are setting a life back on track.

When you dare to care
You take a risk to open your heart
When you dare to care
You give room in your heart to share your today.
When you dare to care
You help to change tomorrow by letting someone into your today,
When you dare to care
Heaven salutes you.

Dedicated to Mr. and Mrs. Oluseye Oyeleye
London, UK.

AN AFRICAN CHILD

From the coasts of West Africa
To the deserts of North Africa
The voices of children cry out
They cry against hunger, injustice,
Neglect, poverty, and abuse
Why does the world not hear their cry?
Yes, I am an African child
Please give me my attention.

From the rivers of East Africa
To the vast lands of South Africa,
I hear the echo of tiny voices
Crying out for papa and mama
Oh the sting of death!
AIDS has snatched them away!
Why this disease?
I feel like punching AIDS right in the face!
How can I face tomorrow with no one to inspire me?
The burden on my shoulders is too great for me.
I am an African child
Please give me my dreams.

From America to Asia,
From Europe to Australia,
Hear the voice of the African child.

To the great leaders of the world;
The African child clings to your round table
Why do I have to be last on the mind of the world?
I am an African child
I need to stand on equal ground.

I can speak and I can read
I am smart and I am courageous
I am bold and I am beautiful
I can be a strong leader
I can dance and play
I laugh and cry
I dream of great things-
I am not dumb and backward
I am an African child
You must hear my voice
Please give me your ears.

I will keep crying even if I lose my voice
My bones will play the drums in your ears
You will see my picture everywhere you go.
I am an African child
I am not asking for your world
I am inviting you into mine.
When you see it, you will know
That I am strong, tough, and courageous
I am not all that you think I am,
I am an African child
Please give me a place in your heart.

CHECK OUT GIRL

Hello . . . smile, scan, pack
Smile, smile, smile
Scan, scan, scan
Pack, pack, pack
Oh, her life on the till.
Well, that's the job of a check out girl.
Hey, jump on that till
Hey, go on your break
Hey, stop chatting!
Orders, orders, orders
Keep shut, the boss is coming
Oh! The orders to a checkout girl.

Some are lazy, some are smart,
Some are tall, some are short
Some know what they want
Some are confused.
Some have cash, some have cards
Some have their wallets
Some have lost it
Some don't want to pay
But will get caught anyway-
So much drama at the tills,
Oh, the visitors of a checkout girl.

Clock in, clock out
Check time, break time
Overtime, more time
Pay day, Christmas day
Oh! The moments of a checkout girl . . .

A checkout girl trying to get by
Just a student trying to get by
Just a mother trying to get by
Just a grandmother trying to survive
Look beyond the smile,
Find a dream for a better tomorrow
Look beyond the uniform,
Find a woman who needs to be respected
A checkout girl on straight shifts
Hoping for a shift in life soon-
Well, that's the dream of a checkout girl.

THE IMMIGRANT

"Enjoy your flight madam"
She heard the hostess say
Thank you, she responded
Deep within her she thought,
What lies ahead of me?
I am going to a foreign land,
Would it be like home?

"Would you like a drink?"
Her thoughts were interrupted
Yes, please.
She mumbled under her breath
Let me drink and cool my throat
She was choking with tears
She remembered her farewell entourage
When will she see them again?
She was carrying their hopes and dreams
A heavy burden on her shoulders.
An unrealistic expectation from her,
A misconception of a new life abroad.

"Enjoy your stay, it is a nice city"
The kind lady said
As she got off the "big bird"
The chilly breeze "slapped" her skin

Penetrating deep into her T-shirt-
Ah! This cold is not like our Harmattan, she mumbled.

"That is a nice name"
The man at the shop said
"But how do you say it?"
She thought; you mean, you can't say my name?
But I can say yours.
She was interrupted again
"So do you have any experience?"
She thought again
Well, I have just arrived
Eh, yes, I can do anything!
Walking out of the shop,
She smiled and said, thank you sir.

FLAME

Keep fanning your flame
Keep your light aflame
In your little corner of the world
Remember the sparks from Docklands
Stratford and the good old Barking-
Sparkle and dazzle
Yes! Make the world marvel.

***Dedicated to Alumni of
The University of East London (UEL), UK.***

(ROOTS)

ON THE WINGS OF HOPE

Hope greets you today-
We are gathered because of a common dream
We are gathered because of a common passion
We are hopeful of our tomorrow
We are free from the shackles of yesterday,
Hope has unlocked our dreams . . .

Our nation stands on hope because you are here,
I feel hope rising . . .
Its crescendo higher than when we first stood on our feet
Independent and liberated
Free to think and act as a people;
Ushered into our possibilities . . .
Yes, I feel hope rising!

Arise and soar on the wings of hope
Arise and glide against the wind of our past
Arise and clinch our freedom . . .
Yes! I feel hope rising from the ashes of despair . . .

The drummers and dancers splash colours of hope
Our rich cultural heritage splash from their hips
The dance of freedom pounding on our land
Yes, hope is dancing . . . .

I feel hope rising as their tempo rises.
Harmony in their melody strikes the chord of unity
One nation, one voice, one hope . . .

In service to the people . . . give the gift of hope
In friendly handshakes . . . give the gift of hope
From the old to the young . . . pass the baton of hope.
Greet your family, friends, and neighbours . . .
In the name of hope.
I feel hope rising . . . I see Nigeria Rising,
Welcome to the Glittering Golden Age!

A Celebration of Nigeria @ 50 1ˢᵗ October 2010

A DELIGHTFUL LAND

Baba . . . Almighty, please we ask for a good land.
May our land stand in your hand-
Bless the sand on our land
May our land be joyful and peaceful
May our land be wealthy and healthy
May we live to enjoy our land . . . Amen.

Oh! Let the celebration be grand for our land!
We celebrate our good hearts
We celebrate our nationhood
We celebrate our rich soil
We celebrate our daily toil
We celebrate our "sweet" oil
Let it boom and not zoom . . .
Let it never be our doom!
May it flow and flow!
May we glow and glow-

May our land be delightful-
A land where sleep is beautiful
A land where life is valued
A land where we are free to believe
A land where we believe and live.
A land where hard work is crowned
A land where the weak is not drowned

A land where children bloom-
May we groom our hope for tomorrow.

This land is our home . . .
Oh, may some come home-
May it always be home, good home
May it always be home, peaceful home
May it always be home, joyful home.
May it always be home, pleasant home
May it always be home, fruitful home
May it always be "*home, sweet home*"
May it never be home, bitter home!
Ah! Papa God, we pray . . . may our land be delightful
Beautiful, wonderful, bountiful, and powerful!

SHAKARA .... PRIDE

When you love your country
When you love your people
When you talk on the street
You will show Shakara!

When you love your culture
When you love your language
When you love your roots
You will show Shakara!

When you love your faith
When you love your hope
When you love the Almighty
You will show Shakara!

When you love your children
When you love your spouse
When you love your family
You will show Shakara!
Good shakara . . .

NIGERIA ... A SALUTE TO COURAGE

The journey is long so we must march on
Tired and discouraged, but we must march on;
We told them we can carry our burden
Yes, they are watching and waiting
But we must march to the finish line
Through the bites of armies of termites and locusts,
Oh, what we have endured
Oh, what we have survived-
The journey of one nation
The struggle of many people
A salute to Nigeria
A salute to courage . . .

Oh Giant! Oh Eagle!
The Giant must be refreshed, refueled, and refined . . .
A Giant does not take baby steps!
Have you seen the strides of a Giant?
Oh, the Eagle will fly again . . .
But right now, we will cry in silence and ache on our beds . . .
Kai
We will wonder and ponder
We will not go yonder-
We will open our eyes and ears
We will open our mind and change
We will learn from the past and from our neighbours

But let them know that we are on a journey and we will survive
The Giant is about to leap!

Oh yes we have fallen, but we have also risen!
We must keep rising . . .
Who would ever think that we will still be one?
Yes, we have oceans and mountains of problems
The scars on our backs are pages of our history
The scars on our faces are engravings of our victory
Remember, we are writing our story . . .
A salute to Nigeria
A salute to Courage . . .

WRAPPER

Akwete clothe, George, Hollandis!
Wrapped in layers or singles
Wrapped around your waist
Wrapped around your hips
Wrapped down to your ankles-
You are wrapped up in your roots
You are wrapped up in elegance.

Oh, my wrapper wraps me up at night!
From my grandma to my mama
From my mama to me
From me to my daughter
Wrapper must be passed on,
Oh wrapper . . . Wrapping generations in roots and
elegance.

THAT GELE

Call it a satellite dish or a food platter
Call it a calabash, a pot or frying pan
Call it a basin, a bucket or a canoe
Call it a mushroom growing on a woman's head!
That gele is a crown of beauty.

She steps in and becomes the centerpiece;
All eyes are on the African woman
Gazes and admiration . . . wondering and guessing
Where is she from?
Aha, that gele is a mouthpiece.

It opens like a dandelion in springtime
Clusters of gele are like roses on a bridal bouquet
That headgear dazzles while they marvel
African princess . . . wear your crown
That gele is a beauty.

Grandma ties it like a damsel
Her gele is exotic and chic
She twists and turns the thing with her feeble hands
As she bends and raises her head . . . Mama is a queen!

That gele is a show stopper and vision stopper!
Stamp your presence with your design

Oh sister, unmask your beauty with that damask
African mama, that gele is superb
With your gele you are on center stage
So forget your worries,
Bend and shuffle to the rhythm.

FETCHING WATER

We gathered at the public tap
Chatting, laughing, and playing
Lifting buckets of water,
Water balanced on your 'oshuka'
At the tap friendships blossomed.

When the taps screeched
We swarm to a well like bees
When one was "slammed,"
We buzzed to another
Sometimes we begged to fetch water-
Water to wash and clean
We waited and waited
Then the "water news" gushed . . .

Fetching water brought out kind hearts
We watered friendships
Laughter poured from our lips . . .
Joy trickled into homes!

TODAY . . . YOUR TOMORROW

A silent pain like a tooth ache
A silent pain like a head ache,
But a silent today will birth a still born.
So we must scream like a woman in labour!
Let today give birth to a bouncing tomorrow of hope!
What is in your today?

But we will not scream with our voices;
Let education and dedication shout
Let honesty, and integrity yell
Let hard work and good works roar
Invest in your today . . .

Let pangs of hunger rain;
Hunger for a better future must strike your mind!
Let the crusade begin-
Let the children dream
Let the youths dream
Let the old give advice . . .
Today is in the "labour room."

MY ROOTS

I wake up from my slumber
And I look in the mirror
I see ebony; pure blackness.
I look at my hair and I look at my eyes
I see the awesome work of His hands
Deeply tanned and deeply happy
I was born and I will live in my shade
My roots in you I am content.

I walk on the streets and I see my world
I see my challenges and I see my fears
I see my struggles and my mountains
But I also see my strength and my virtue
Deeply tanned and deeply happy
My life is filled with so much colours of happiness
My roots, my blackness . . . my pride and my joy
My roots . . . not a mistake.

OKAZI SOUP

Precious green leaves thinly diced
In aromatic and creamy soup
Mouth watering and finger licking-
This delicacy, my native delicacy
My mother's delicacy, a family delicacy
Oh! Okazi soup.

Going from house to house
Exchanging pleasantries
Happy chatty children
Visiting old aunts and uncles
Hoping to eat some Okazi soup.

Festivals and special seasons
Okazi soup should grace your menu
Akpu, pounded yam, eba must sit side by side,
Dry fish, isam, meat, stock fish
Must all meet in the pot!
Ofe Okazi . . . hmm Okazi Soup.

LOVE

THE HEART

They say, follow your heart . . .
I say, which heart?
This heart which could be unstable
This heart which could be desperately wicked
This heart which sometimes does not know what it wants!
But I know the heart that I will ask for;
The heart of my heavenly father.
That is the heart that I will follow-
The heart that is full of love
The heart that knows my heart
The heart that knows all hearts
That is the model heart.

Yes, love makes the heart ache
Yes, love makes the heart break
Yes, love makes the heart alive
Yes, love makes the heart strong
The heart is truly the core of our being
The heart is truly the core of our life
Guard the heart . . . guard your life.

STRAYING HEART

O thank you lord for rescuing
This straying heart,
O how it wandered beyond your boundaries
O how it dwelt in a strange land-
But not too far for your loving hand.

Thank you for mercy and grace
Like loving sisters they reached out,
With gentle and tender arms
They snatched me away from harm's way-
Peace and joy embraced me
They wrapped me up like a new born baby
Swaddled in its crib.

Thank you for bringing me into my vineyard-
You were preparing it all along
O how blind I was.

May I help a sister find her way
May I help one who has gone astray
May she find peace in your boundaries for love
Yes, may our hearts not stray into a strange land.

LOVE IS A SEED

Is love about roses, chocolates, and perfumes?
Is love about diamonds, pearls, and gold?
Is love about a Porsche or a Prado?
A little of these might show you care
But Love is a seed so choose what you sow.

Some tiny seeds bring huge fruits
Some huge seeds bring tiny fruits
Some seeds don't grow into tall plants
Some seeds don't have beautiful flowers
Each seed has a reason to live,
So think of your fruit and sow your seed.

Each seed needs time to grow
Each seed needs care to grow
Each seed needs sunshine to blossom
Each seed needs a good soil to bloom
So pray that your seed will find the right soil.
Love is a seed . . . . sow it right.

THE MISSING RIB

Sound asleep one lonely night
Alone for the last time tonight
He slept with all his ribs in place
Awoke with one missing rib
How wonderful
How beautiful
For one missing rib,
No longer will I be lonely.

My wife, the bone of my bones
I have found my missing rib in you
The flesh of my flesh
Never will you be a thorn in my flesh.
One missing rib brought forth you and
You brought forth a whole new world,
Find your missing rib and
Find your New World.

I DO

Dressed in white,
Sparkling in white,
Smiling and glittering
Princess of the day!
Glow to the Altar
And say I do.
Say I do, to the one you love.

Snap, snap, snap,
Flash, flash, flash,
Many faces, many places.
Keeping your cool
Looking so cool
Needing something cool;
To cool your thirst.
It is a cool day but you are hot!
Saying I do sure can make you hot!
I do: wow . . . what lies ahead?

I do . . . to a new future
I do . . . to a new life
I do . . . to a new tomorrow
I do . . . because it is you and I trust you
I do . . . because you can do what you said
I do . . . because God has His eyes on us
I do . . . for so many reasons, I don't know all, but
I do . . . because Love and Faith brought us here.

LOVE LIFTED ME

On the journey of love
I stumbled and I fell
Rejection made me stoop and cry
But your love gave me wings to fly
Yes, love lifted me.

Your kind words
Your gentleness
Your outstretched arms,
Your patience
Your faith and confidence in me
All made me soar high
Yes, love lifted me.

Sweet love for a queen
Sweet love for a princess
Sweet love for a damsel
Sweet love for a pauper!
Every woman needs that sweet love
Sweet love lifted me!
Now, I am flying on eagle's wings.
Glory, Halleluyah!

PLACES & SIGHTS

BUS STOPS (London, England)

Kisses and hugs
Smoking and drinking
Oh no!
Quarrels and chats
Giggles and laughs
Oh! So much drama at bus stops.

Bus Number . . .
368, 387, 257, 238
362,181,124,185
Watch out your bus is coming,
Watch out you may catch the wrong bus
Watch out, the driver may not stop,
Run, run, run,
Bang, bang, bang
Stop driver!
Oh . . . so much drama at bus stops.

Wait wait wait
In summer, winter,
Autumn, and spring
Some fish and chips
Some chicken and chips,
A pound for a meal
A pound for my bus fare
Tough choices at bus stops.

AWESOME HANDS ... NIAGARA

Water, rushing waters
I see your force and I shiver
I can't see your beginning—mighty waters
How awesome are the hands that made you.

Great Niagara Falls
Created between two great countries,
I stand in Niagara, Canada
And I see Niagara, New York
Oh! Awesome hands have made me.
Great Niagara Falls,
What a wonder!

NAKED TREES

In spring the leaves are green
Showered with lots of sheen
Swaying endlessly
From branch to branch,
Oh, happy and proud tree.

Then autumn comes and strips her!
But first, she is draped in
Radiant red, yelling yellow,
Bubbling brown, opulent orange
Pretty purple and brilliant burgundy!

Then the leaves drop-
Tumbling and rolling
Alas the tree is naked
Unwrapped for winter-
It will shiver and quiver in the snow!

MOLUE

Big and yellow with black stripes
Big and high above the ground
"King" of the road!
Open doors
Open windows
Rusty and rugged
Ah, Molue!

Men and women hanging on the door
Men and women standing on the aisle
Boys and girls jumping in and out
Ah! Molue!

Shouting drivers
Fighting bus conductors
"Madam, I no get change oh"
"Oga pay me my money oh"
Ah! Molue

Buyers and sellers take their stand
Fighters and peacemakers take their seats
Teachers and preachers speak the truth
Medicine and snack sellers take their spots
Molue, you carry precious lives.
Molue the face of Eko . . . Lagos.

MILE 2

Aha, the arrival and departure place
Bus stop for many journeys . . .
Buses and taxis to Ghana, Cotonu, Badagry, Ibadan
Any where . . . .
Board the ferry to Wharf or take a little cruise to an island
Just get to Mile 2 and you will find your way.
Ah! Eko.

Hawkers and roadside sellers
Shoe makers and blacksmiths
Drivers and conductors
Mama Put and pepper soup joints
Walking bridges converted to shopping stalls
Overhead bridges converted to sleeping stalls
Busy roads with no traffic lights
Chaos on every side
Noise, noise and more noise
Welcome to Mile 2!

Estates and fine houses,
Mansions and flats
Rich and poor
Ibo, Yoruba, Hausa, Efik . . . all tribes
Mile 2 is for everybody

Mile 2 is for the old and young
Mile 2 is for the big and small
Mile 2 is a business centre
Come and buy Aroso rice
When you see Mile 2, it is really Lagos na wah!

Surrounded by Festac, Okota,
Maza Maza and Oshodi expressway
Mile 2 stands tall.
You must greet her before you go to Okoko and Barracks
Satellite town and Agbara
You might also see her on your way to the airport
Ah! Mile 2, you need to shine.
Aha, all eyes are on you!

A RAINY DAY IN LAGOS

The waters are pounding the roofs
The waters are pounding the ground
The rain is flogging everything!
Even umbrellas are "running" for cover.

People huddled in shelters
Children cuddled on backs and arms
Trendy hikers in shower caps
Gears for the sky taps-

Cars slither like snails-
Go-slow!
Bumper to bumper
Side to side
Everybody will get "somewhere,"
"Somehow," soon.
Everybody understands,
On a rainy day, Lagos crawls!

THE GARDEN CITY

The city where almost everything happens off "Aba road"
The city where almost everyone lives in "Rumu" something
The city where almost everybody "knows" everybody!
A small city with the "big pocket"
The garden city . . .

Mile 1, mile 2, mile 3, mile 4, mile 5, mile . . .
The small city with many miles
My roots are in these miles
I walked miles to school-
Stopping to watch goats in labour at Chinda's compound
Stopping to admire horses grazing on the polo field at "GRA"
Stopping to admire houses with almond trees and "beware of dogs"
Stopping to pluck almond fruits and racing for my life!
My heart is racing to my first city.

The city with lush lawns in "GRA" and "oil Camp"
The city with "triumphant" bus stops;
Artillery, Garrison, Air force base, Oil mill,
Presidential, Park, Waterline, Rainbow . . .

My garden city-My first city
A city to protect
A city to respect
*(GRA-Government Residential Area)

ABULOMA

Girls dressed in white shirts
Wine colored pinafores or skirts
Running from the dinning hall to the dormitory
Dressed in sports shorts and t-shirts
Running from the dormitory to the classroom
And then off to the games field
Abuloma, my memories are running all over.

Sitting with my plate and cutlery
Hoping that someone does not take it and fail to return it
Hoping that my meal portion is a good size today
Hoping that I could go home and eat something different
Hoping . . . just hoping that I have enough water to drink
Hoping that I don't have to run just after my meal,
Abuloma, I hope to see you again someday.

Night preps and noon preps
Exams and tests
Assignments and assessments
First three, 70% and above, last three
End of term results, awards and speeches.
Abuloma, you helped to train young minds

You helped to sharpen dull minds
You helped to make timid ones bold
Abuloma, many are the daughters you have raised.

Friends, friends, friends
Forever found and kept because we sucked from your breast
Precious memories of lives touched and held
Precious moments of joy and laughter
Abuloma, you are my treasure.

I hope the foundation is still strong
I hope the teachers are well and happy
I hope the buildings are smooth and clean
I hope the chairs, tables, and beds are enough for all.
I see beautiful dormitory colours . . . .
I see Jasmine, Primrose, Bluebell, Allamanda and Lavender
I see Ixora and Lily
I smell okro soup
I smell egusi soup
Somebody please tell me I heard the dinning bell!
Yes, I don't like the rising bell!
Oh Abuloma . . . I laugh whenever I think of you.

MOTHERHOOD

JUST A BABY

He tells me when to sleep
He tells me when to wake up
He tells me when to eat
He tells me to give him all the attention,
Yes, he's just a baby.

She tells me when to go out
She tells me when to stay in
She tells me when to take a shower
My life has been turned around
I surrender,
Yes, she is just a baby.

A baby will change your life
A baby will make you soft
A baby will make you tender and sweet
A baby will also make you hungry and tired
When they arrive in your world, they take charge!
He or she, yes . . . just a baby,
A special gift to you.

MAMA LOVES YOU

As you suckle, snuggle, and cuddle,
I thank God for giving me
The most precious gift of all . . .
A little one!
I touch your head and count
Your tiny toes and fingers
And wrap you like a ball
My little pumpkin
Mama loves you.

It seems like only yesterday
I wondered . . . . would it be a boy or a girl?
You kicked in my tummy
You wiggled in my belly
You made me restless
I promised to pinch you when I see you;
But now I am mellow like a pillow
You are more than I thought
Let me enjoy your baby days
'Cause I know it will fly away so quickly,
Mama loves you.

SOMETIMES I WONDER

Sometimes I wonder how so much noise
Can come from such a little one,
Sometimes I wonder why you have to cry for everything;
For food, to sleep, for a change, to be carried, when you wake up,
I just wonder . . . say it babe
Then I remember, they don't talk that early.

Sometimes I wonder who you really look like,
What will you be in future?
How will your voice sound?
I hope you will love my cooking . . .
Sometimes, I just wonder . . .

Sometimes I wonder how you learn so fast
I wonder how you grow so fast
I wonder if you know just how much you are loved
And how much you mean to me
I wonder if you know how precious you are to me
Sometimes I just wonder . . .

LOVE IS LIKE A BABY

Love is like a baby
It takes time to grow.
Premature, due or overdue,
A baby will brighten your life,
so will love.

Love is like a baby
Crawling, standing, walking, and running,
It takes time to learn, and they fall and cry
So is love.

Love is like a baby
Sometimes you can not figure out all they want
But you hang in there and hope that you are doing it right.
So is love: Love endures all things.

Love is like a baby
Sometimes you feel like taking a break
When they become cranky and messy,
But when they smile and melt your heart
You thank God that you have someone special
So is love, there are some tough times
But you are blessed to have someone to love you,
We all have messy moments, but love stays close.

Love is like a baby
Trusting you completely that you will be there
Looking up to you for help,
Believing that mummy and daddy are the best,
So is love, you have got to trust and believe in what you
have.

Love is like a baby,
Always wants to be cuddled, carried and tickled
They always want to be touched
So is love: a hug, a kiss just to say I love you
And I am here for you,
Babies love attention, and so does love.

I NEED YOU

I have never known this road before
I have never known this role before
I will ever open my heart to learn,
Lord please teach me how to be a mother
I need you Lord to be a "mama."

When I am angry, please calm me down
When I am anxious please give me peace
When I am overwhelmed please give me grace
When I am tired please be my strength.
When I am sad please fill me with your joy
When I don't know what to do, I will look up to you
Lord I need you to be a "mama."

Give me patience to say things over and over
Give me more laughter to understand a child.
Teach me how to tickle and cuddle
Teach me how to giggle and wiggle
Teach me the heart of a child
Lord I need you to be a "mama."

IN YOUR EYES MY SWEET SON

I look into your beautiful and gorgeous eyes,
All I see is pure Innocence.
Staring at me . . . "tell me all I need to know mama
I am counting on you."
In your eyes, I see truth, trust and peace
My baby, grow into a man and do keep those eyes,
I will always look into your eyes.

When I look into your eyes
Suddenly, I feel all my path led to you;
They were long and narrow with many crossroads
But I am glad I did not miss you.
In your eyes, I see a better tomorrow,
Please be better than we are
In your eyes my sweet son, I see a strong champion.

A MOTHER'S HEART

A treasure of strength
A well of compassion
A fountain of grace
An ocean of patience
A mother's heart is rich
A mother's heart is priceless.

A mother's heart beats with rhythms of love and care
A mother's heart has silent melodies of hope
A mother's heart is a gem,
A mother's heart makes many happy hearts.

ADA

My little madam
My little miss
My cutie pie
My Ada . . .
You are the first girl in my life.

The way you walk
The way you smile
The way you giggle
The way you swing your arms
Ah! Ada, you are truly the first lady.

You are blessed
You are brilliant
You are beautiful
You are my beloved Ada.

When I look at you
I pray for virtue as you grow
When I look at you
I pray for courage to live right.
When I look at you
I know you will make us proud
Oh, Ada . . . . You are the queen of the house.

CHRISTMAS

IT IS CHRISTMAS

It is not all about stopping and shopping,
It is about stopping and caring.
It is not about stuffing and getting
It is about sharing and giving.
It is Christmas, what are you stopping and doing?

It is not about new dresses and shoes
It is about new dreams and souls.
It is not about parties and dinners
It is about passion and divinity
It is Christmas, which virtues are you wearing?

It is Christmas . . . Hearts are open
It is Christmas . . . Homes are open
It is Christmas . . . Halleluyah, Halleluyah.

SWEET MOTHER OF JESUS

Humble, gentle, and faithful-
Mary took the angel's message with grace and fear.
"Be it unto me according to thy word."
How did you feel knowing you will be the greatest mother?
Sweet mother of Jesus.

When you gave the baby Jesus a bath each day
To wash away his dirt from playing
Did you know that one day He will wash away your sins?
When you cooked his favourite meal
And watched him clean his plate
Did you know that He is the bread of Life?
And He would feed thousands of people with just five loaves
and two fishes.

When you watched Him play
And protected Him from falls, hurts, and wounds,
Did you know that He is your refuge, your healer, and your
guide?
When you taught him to touch His nose, eyes, and mouth
Did you know that He created you?
And He will give the blind their sight
And make the dumb speak!
Oh, sweet mother . . . you loved your son, the Son of God.

When you lost him at the Passover feast
And you thought you had failed at your job

Did you know that He is the light of life and will find His way back?

Did you know that He came to find the lost?

When you watched Him become a carpenter like Joseph

Did you know that He can do all things?

Did you know that He is also a king?

When you gave Him water to drink

Did you know that He is the fountain of living waters?

And if you drink of Him you will thirst no more.

Did you know that He will also calm the storm and walk on water?

Sweet Mother of Jesus . . .

You are blessed to be called mama by the creator of all things.

HIS BIRTHDAY

It is His birthday
But you did not invite Him.
It is His special day
But He has got no place to call His own
How would you feel, if you were in His shoes?

It is His birthday
But you have invited only your friends.
It is His big day
But He gets no attention
How would you feel, if you were in His shoes?

It is His birthday
And you do not know much about Him
It is His stage but you have got all eyes on you.
Do you care about Him or what He likes?
It is Christmas . . . do you know the Christ?

WHERE IS THE TRUE LIGHT?

Streets and trees are shining and sparkling
Walls and roofs are glittering and stunning
The night is alive and the lights are awake;
But where is the true light that shines in our heart?

Shops and malls are filled with lights
Offices and towers sparkle and dazzle
A drive at night feels like day with all the lights;
But where is the true light that shines in our hearts?

The light that tells me to love my neighbour
The light that tells me to stop the hatred
The light that leads me to lend a hand
The light that shines in the darkest heart
The light that drives the gun away;
That is the light that should shine today
When will you light up your heart?

BABY JESUS

He suckled and He was cuddled
He cried and He was carried
Baby Jesus, oh baby Jesus.

Nursed by Mary and watched by many
He crawled, walked, and talked
Baby Jesus, oh baby Jesus.

My king and my master
He came as a baby to live in my world
He came as a baby to feel my pain
When I see Him, I will be like a baby
Crying in endless worship
Let my heart be soft like a baby.

CHRISTMAS IS DEAR TO ALL

Family from far and near
Friends from far and near
Stories from far and near,
Christmas is dear to all.

Memories of care to share
Memories so dear to hear
Memories of joy and hope,
Christmas is dear to all.

Amidst the eating and drinking
Amidst the cooking and cleaning
Amidst the packing and traveling.
Amidst the calls and visits
Amidst the shopping and shopping
Amidst the gifts and gestures,
Let us pause for the reason for the season-
Jesus is dear to all
Christmas is dear to all.

LIFE

THE DREAM

A silent pain
A nurtured thought
The cry of my heart.
In my little fantasy island
My secret world
My treasured desires
The sun will soon set
Upon the Dream.

The clock may tick fast
But my vision will not die
The flame will not quench
I was born to do it, be it and
I will see it come true
I have a dream;
Yes I am living the dream.

YOUR LIFE SHOULD COUNT

Seasons and reasons
People and places
Moments and comments
Life is indeed full of these,
But your life should count.

Setbacks and comebacks
Valleys and mountains
Tough times and happy times
Sweet things and bitter things,
But in all, your life should count.

You can touch a life
You can reach out today
You can wipe a tear
You can give a smile
At the end of this age,
Your life should count.

SOMETIMES

Do you know that the rejected,
Would be looked for one day?
Do you know that the despised
Would be looked for one day?
Do you know that the disappointed
Would be looked for one day?
Sometimes in life,
The story is not yet over when you think it is.

Do you know that today is the tomorrow you prayed for
yesterday?
Do you know this moment is yours to cherish?
Do you know that this time is yours to invest?
Do you know that this man is yours to love?
Do you know that this woman is yours to love?
Do you know that this child is yours to nurture and love?
Sometimes in life, we need to value more what we have.

Sometimes we do not get all that we ask
God gives us just what we need
Sometimes we do not understand all that we see
God makes all things beautiful in His time,
We need to make all "sometimes" His time.

LONDON LIFE

Markets and shops
Fish and chips
Chicken and chips
Tubes and trains
Black cabs and red buses.
That's London's sights
Well, that's London life.

Bills, bills, bills
Work, work, work
Hurry, hurry, hurry
Oh! What a life
Oh! That's Western life
Well, that's London Life

Tax, Tax, Tax
Take, take, take
Give, Give, Give
Buy, buy, buy
Spend, spend, spend
Oh, what a drained life
Well, that's London life.

Rain, rain, rain
Sunny, rainy, sunny
Rainy, sunny, rainy
Snowy, rainy, sunny

Cold, hot, cold
Aha! Make up your mind weather
Well, that's London's headache
That's London Life.

Chinese, Jamaican, Turkish
Indian, Nigerian, Pakistan,
Swedish, Italian, Japanese,
Kenyan, Ghanaian, English
American, Iraqi, Israeli . . .
Well, that's London's people
Yes, that's London life.

COLD LAND

Shivering and stammering
This cold bites into my bones
How can this be?
-35 degrees centigrade!
Oh lord, I need your help
This cold land . . . How can it be?

Piles of white-
Roof tops and car tops
Sidewalks and slow walks.
Dressed from head to toe
Dressed from month to month
Aha! This cold land, dressed in white.

Snow storms and black ice
Foggy sky and slippery ground
Long coats and thick hats
Long boots and thick shoes
Thick gloves and thick scarves
Gears for the cold land . . .

Frost bites and stiff ears
Dry lips and dry legs
Cracked skin and rough hands-
Bites in a cold "slamming" land!

Some coffee to keep you warm
Some heat to keep you warm
Hot soup for your stomach
Hot soup to keep you warm
O Maple leaf land!

FAMILY

WHAT JOY

Sitting together eating and laughing
Sleeping together, just yapping and napping
Little moments . . . precious moments
What joy it is to have a family.

Taking a long drive
Taking a long walk
Chatting and planning
Praying and planning
What joy it is to have a family.

Praying together
Worshipping together
Crying together
Caring and sharing moments
Loving and tender moments
Oh what joy it is to have a family.

MY AUNTY

I traveled from the west to the east
No money to go back to the west
A struggling student I was,
But you were there for me
Always providing
My Aunty, how I miss you so much.

You did not have much
But you gave so much
You gave your best
So I could have the best
My Aunty, how I miss you so much
There was always a hot pot of soup
Whenever I was hungry,
A cold expensive drink to quench my thirst
Times when I was sad, you made me laugh
You showed me off to your friends and neighbours
Your pride and joy as you sang my praise.

I remember us walking down the road
As I made my way to the bus station,
Hand in hand we walked
And you gave me precious words of wisdom.
I can still feel those gentle arms
Wrapped around my shoulders
I can still see your face and arms
Waving goodbye and saying . . .

I will be here when you come again,
Now you have traveled far away
Not to the east or west, but far beyond
I did not get a chance to say goodbye.

Some nights, I cry
But I know you feel no more pain from sickness
But only love in the master's arms.
I was looking forward to bringing you goodies,
Goodies from the white man's land
To say thank you for being there for me.
But I know up in heaven
You have better goodies . . . . peace and freedom from pain
I look forward to telling you stories and hugging you so close
I know one day we will meet again,
Oh my Aunty, how I miss you so much.

OH GRANDMA! THAT CALL

Many miles away
Grandma "whispers" on the phone
When will I see your face?
When will I see my children?
When are you coming home?

Ah! grandma, please wait for us
Please don't go "anywhere"
We are coming to see you.

Hmm, the journey abroad is far-
Aged ones loved and missed,
Hoping and longing to unite
When the "pocket" is right
Just wishing that they will be there
To embrace whenever you return
Oh, this sojourning.

But grandma did not wait
She went to "sleep" . . .
That call was our goodbye
That call, oh that call.
Her voice echoes in my head;
That call captured it . . .
Sleep well, Grandma.

BLESSED HANDS

Her precious hands are soft and tender
Her precious hands are smooth and slender
Hands that wash the dishes
Hands that wash the babies
Hands that cook and sew
Hands that bake and look for things to make,
Her hands are busy hands
Her hands are blessed hands
Yes, that is mother's hands!

Her hands are tools of affectionate touches
Her hands do what her heart says
Her hands are for hugs, cuddles, and tickles
Her hands are also for smacks and serving my snacks,
Her hands are always open for a warm embrace.

Mother's hands are a gift to her family
Mother's hands are a treasure in her home
Mother's hands speak!
Look around and you will see . . .
Mother's hands are blessed
And I am blessed because she touched me.

GLOSSARY

Abuloma: A town in Rivers State, Nigeria, where a prestigious girls' high school is located—Federal Government Girls' College, Abuloma.

Ada: The name given to the first daughter in the Ibo tribe in Nigeria.

Akpu: White solid meal made from processed cassava.

Akwete Clothe: A specially crafted wrapper produced by the people of Akwete, Ndoki in Abia State, Nigeria.

Aroso: A brand of long grain rice.

Broad Street: A busy downtown street in Lagos, Nigeria.

Cotonou: Country capital of the Republic of Benin.

Eba: A meal made from processed cassava, used for eating native soup.

Egusi soup: A soup made with melon seeds.

Eko: A common name for the city of Lagos.

Gele: Headgear in Yoruba language.

Ghana: A West African country.

*Harmattan:*The cold and dry season in Nigeria

Ibadan: The capital of Oyo State, Nigeria.

Isam: (Periwinkle In Ibo) Seafood used in native soups

Molue: A classic public transportation bus in the city of Lagos.

Mile 2 Jakande: A low cost housing estate in the city of Lagos.

Ofe: Soup in the Ibo language.

Okazi: An indigenous green leaf used for soups.

Okro: A vegetable used for making soup.

Oshuka: A piece of cloth rolled and placed on the head to balance a bucket of water.

Pounded yam: A solid meal used to eat soup.

Shakara: A fun word used to describe pride in Nigeria.

Local

Mama put: A fun name used to describe the owner of a local eatery specializing in native delicacies. Most of these eateries are owned and managed by women.

Madam, I no get change oh: Lady I do not have change.

Na wah / kai: Exclamations.

Oga pay me my money oh: Mr. Pay your fare.

Pepper soup joints: Local eateries specializing in cooking goat, fish, and chicken soup, with lots of hot spices. These are also regular chatting places for people living in the community.